~~Deb McClintock~~
W9-AXR-422

A Note to Parents

Dorling Kindersley Readers is a compelling new program for beginning readers, designed in conjunction with leading literacy experts, including Dr. Linda Gambrell, President of the National Reading Conference and past board member of the International Reading Association.

Beautiful illustrations and superb full-color photographs combine with engaging, easy-to-read stories to offer a fresh approach to each subject in the series. Each *Dorling Kindersley Reader* is guaranteed to capture a child's interest while developing his or her reading skills, general knowledge, and love of reading.

The four levels of *Dorling Kindersley Readers* are aimed at different reading abilities, enabling you to choose the books that are exactly right for your child:

Level 1 – Beginning to read
Level 2 – Beginning to read alone
Level 3 – Reading alone
Level 4 – Proficient readers

The "normal" age at which a child begins to read can be anywhere from three to eight years old, so these levels are intended only as a general guideline.

No matter which level you select, you can be sure that you are helping your child learn to read, then read to learn!

Dorling Kindersley

LONDON, NEW YORK, SYDNEY, DELHI, PARIS,
MUNICH, and JOHANNESBURG

A DORLING KINDERSLEY BOOK
www.dk.com

Produced by Southern Lights
Custom Publishing

For Dorling Kindersley
Publisher Andrew Berkhut
Executive Editor Andrea Curley
Art Director Tina Vaughan
Photographer Keith Harrelson

Reading Consultant
Linda Gambrell, Ph.D.

First American Edition, 2001
00 01 02 03 04 05 10 9 8 7 6 5 4 3 2 1
Published in the United States by Dorling Kindersley Publishing, Inc.
95 Madison Avenue, New York, New York 10016

Copyright © 2001 Dorling Kindersley Limited, London

All rights reserved under International and Pan-American Copyright Conventions. No part of this publication may be reproduced, stored in a retrieval system, or transmitted in any form or by any means, electronic, mechanical, photocopying, recording, or otherwise, without the prior written permission of the copyright owner.

Published in Great Britain by Dorling Kindersley Limited.

Library of Congress Cataloging-in-Publication Data

Hayward, Linda.
A day in the life of a teacher / by Linda Hayward.-
1st American ed.
p. cm. -- (Dorling Kindersley readers)
Audience: "Level, preschool-grade 1."
ISBN 0-7894-7368-2 ISBN 0-7894-7367-4 (pbk.)
1. Elementary school teachers--Juvenile literature. 2. Elementary school teaching--Juvenile literature. [1.Teachers 2. Schools 3. Occupations.] I. Title. II. Series.

LB1776 H39 2001
372.11--dc21

00-055522

Printed and bound in China by L. Rex Printing Co., Ltd.

The characters and events in this story are fictional and do not represent real persons or events. The author would like to thank Janis Liss for her help.

see our complete
catalog at

www.dk.com

DORLING KINDERSLEY *READERS*

BEGINNING 1 TO READ

A Day in the Life of a Teacher

Written by Linda Hayward

Warsaw Community Public Library
310 East Main Street
Warsaw, IN 46580
(574) 267-6011

A Dorling Kindersley Book

7:00 a.m.

It is time to go to school.
The Hill family gets ready.
Eric and Jason finish breakfast.
Jan Hill fills her tote bag.

Two books,
one lunch,
28 toy fish!

tote bag

Jan teaches second grade.

Jan drives to school.

In the office she
checks her mailbox.
She picks up her
attendance folder.

folder

Time to fix
the calendar!
Today is
Wednesday.

calendar

Before school,
Josh shows
Ms. Hill
his turtle.

Josh was
in her class
last year.

8:00 a.m.
The bell rings.
"Line up here!" says Ms. Hill.
Room Nine lines up.

As they come in, the students put their homework in the basket.

basket

Ms. Hill takes attendance. Ryan is absent.

Hana's reading group practices listening skills.

The class is learning
about fish.
Ms. Hill passes out
the toy fish.
Then she writes a
word on the board.

dictionary

Who can find it in the dictionary?

Brnng!
The fire alarm!
The class lines up
to go outside.

Walking in line
can be hard.

"No pushing!"
says Ms. Hill.

Is it safe to go
back in? Yes!
It was just
a fire drill.

Back in the room, Todd studies spelling words.

Emily reads from her journal.

Ms. Hill asks the aide, Ms. Lee, to cut paper for art. "We need 28 of each!" she says. Ms. Hill is planning a bulletin board.

12:00 p.m.

The teachers have lunch together.
They plan their school show.

"The third grade can sing the song about the forest," says Ms. Lopez.

12:30 p.m.

Lunch is over.
A hush falls in Room Nine.
Ms. Hill is reading
a new book of poems.

Now it is time for math.
Ms. Hill has a box.
She takes out one big red square,
one big yellow circle,
and one small yellow circle.

What other shapes are inside?

1:45 p.m.

Jim and Katy learn about graphs.

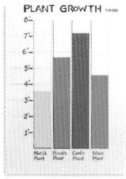

graph

Jose is working on the computer.

Rob has his octopus ready for the bulletin board.

The school day is almost over. The students pack up their homework.

3:00 p.m.

When the bell rings, everyone walks out to the buses.

Ryan's sister comes to pick up his homework. Here is a card that Ryan made for Ms. Hill.

4:30 p.m.

Jan Hill has her own homework. Her son Eric helps with the laundry.

Jason serves dinner. It was his turn to cook.

10:00 p.m.

Before she goes to bed,
Jan looks at
Ryan's card again.

She smiles.
She has the best job in the world!

Picture Word List

tote bag

page 4

dictionary

page 12

folder

page 7

journal

page 16

calendar

page 8

square

page 23

basket

page 10

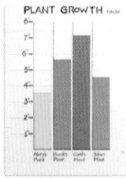

graph

page 24

APR 2 4 2002

J E 372.11 H427d 2001
Hayward, Linda.
A day in the life of a
teacher /

WITHDRAWN